WELCOME TO HOLLAND

A pictorial tour of Holland – what could be easier than that? Tulips, cheese and windmills, and the colourful picture is complete – isn't it? In reality Holland is much more colourful, much richer and much more multi-facetted than the usual clichés would have us believe.

In fact everything we generally associate with Holland is to be found in the two provinces of Zuid-Holland and Noord-Holland. So our pictorial journey will be above all a journey to these two provinces and their sights – the old towns and cheese markets, the blooming bulb fields and the numerous windmills. But also the water, without which Holland is difficult to imagine. No other European country has been so shaped by the water, is still threatened by it, as the Kingdom of the Netherlands. For this is the real, official name of the country. And nowhere in the world have people literally held their ground against the water and the sea as they have done here. "God created the sea, the Frisians created the land." This proud motto of the Frisians high up in the north of the country could easily be applied to the whole of Holland. The dam between Noord-Holland and Friesland, or what has been accomplished in the delta area of the Schelde and Rhine are just two outstanding examples.

Wherever you look in Holland you see water. Rivers that sluggishly roll on towards the North Sea, branching more and more as they go. Canals that forge links between them, making even the furthest corners of the country navigable. Again and again the sea has overrun the land in terrifying storm floods

WILLKOMMEN IN HOLLAND

Eine Farbbildreise durch Holland, das scheint ganz einfach. Tulpen, Käse und Windmühlen, das Hollandbild ist bunt und schnell fertig. Doch in Wirklichkeit ist Holland noch viel farbiger,
Tatsächlich ist all das, was wir gemeinhin uns unter Holland vorstellen, vor allem in den beiden Provinzen Zuid-Holland und Noord-Holland zu finden. Deshalb wird die Bilderreise insbesondere eine Reise zu diesen beiden Provinzen mit ihren Sehenswürdigkeiten sein: den alten Städten und Käsemärkten, den blühenden Tulpenfeldern und den vielen Windmühlen.
Kein anderes Land Europas ist so vom Wasser geprägt und nach wie vor bedroht wie das Königreich der Niederlande. So lautet ja der eigentliche, der offizielle Name für Holland. Und wohl nirgends auf der Welt haben Menschen sich behauptet wie hier. „Gott schuf das Meer, der Friese das Land." Der Abschluß-deich zwischen Noord-Holland und Friesland oder das Deltawerk im Mündungsbereich von Schelde und Rhein sind nur zwei besonders herausragende Beispiele dafür.
Wohin man schaut in Holland, sieht man Wasser. Ströme, die sich träge und immer weiter auseinanderfransend der Nordsee entgegenwälzen. Kanäle, die sie miteinander verbinden und das ganze Land bis in seine entlegensten Winkel zu einem Schiffahrtsland machen. Und immer wieder ist in verheerenden Sturmflutkatastrophen das Meer ins Land eingebrochen, hat weite Landstriche oft für Jahrhunderte unter Wasser gesetzt. Immer wieder haben die Holländer versucht, das Wasser aus dem Land hinauszubringen.

BIENVENUE EN HOLLANDE

Pour présenter la Hollande, les images qui viennent aussitôt à l'esprit sont celles de tulipes, de moulins et de fromages. On a ainsi décrit rapidement un pays pittoresque et haut en couleurs. Mais en réalité, la Hollande a bien plus de facettes que les clichés qui lui sont attachés.
La Hollande possède naturellement tout ce que nous lui associons, notamment en Hollande-Méridionale et Hollande-Septentrionale. Voilà pourquoi nous nous attarderons dans ces deux provinces pour y découvrir les villes anciennes et les marchés aux fromages, les immenses champs de tulipes et les nombreux moulins.
Mais l'eau joue également un rôle primordial en Hollande. Aucun autre pays en Europe n'est dominé et encore menacé par cet élément comme le royaume des Pays-Bas, ainsi que la Hollande s'appelle officiellement. Et nulle part dans le monde, les Hommes ne sont parvenus à vaincre la mer comme ici: «Dieu a créé la mer, les Frisons ont bâti la terre.» Ce fier dicton des habitants du nord du pays s'applique à toutes les régions de Hollande. La digue de fermeture entre la Hollande-Septentrionale et la Frise ou les deltas artificiels aux embouchures de l'Escaut et du Rhin ne sont que des exemples de l'œuvre formidable des Hollandais.
L'eau est présente partout en Hollande. Des fleuves paisibles roulent leurs eaux vers la mer du Nord et se ramifient en chemin. Des réseaux de canaux navigables sillonnent le pays jusque dans ses coins les plus reculés. Et danger constant, des tempêtes provoquent des inon-

オランダ

カラー写真によるオランダ旅行、これは、とても簡単に思える。チューリップ、チーズ、風車に代表されるオランダは、多彩、簡単。ところが、実際のオランダは、もっと多彩で包括的である。事実、オランダのイメージは、特に、南ホーラント州と北ホーラント州に集約されている。それで、これから、この2地方の見処を紹介する。古い町、チーズ市場、咲き乱れるチューリップ畑、沢山の風車。そして水。この水なしにはオランダは、考えられない。ヨーロッパでこの国ほど水の影響が強く、危険にさらされている国は他にない。低地国、これが元来のオランダの正式名である。この国の人々ほど水と、海と戦ってきた国民は他にいない。「神は海を創りフリース人が陸を創った。」と、北オランダのフリース地方の人々はそういって、慰めているのであって、この言葉は全オランダにいえるのである。北ホーランド州とフリースランド州の境界線になっている堤防や、スケルデ川とライン川の河口のデルタ地帯は、これが顕著に現れている。オランダのどこを見ても、北海と繋がっている水や河がある。そして、国の隅々まで運河が通り、一番辺鄙なところにまで、船で行かれるようになっている。何度も暴風雨で海水が陸を襲い、陸が海面下になり、国境線が変わってしまった。

何度もオランダ人は、排水を試みた。海との辛抱強い戦いで、陸地の多くを再獲得した。全フレーボランドはかつては海の下にあったのである。他の処でも、国が、海面以下にあるため、オランダ人は、唯堤防で守られているからのみ生活出来ているのである。毎日、アムステルダムにある世界各国の飛行機が着陸するオランダのスキポール国際空港は、海面以下にある。けれども、

and submerged whole tracts of land, sometimes for centuries. The Dutch have tried again and again to drive the water out of their country. In a dogged battle they have wrested many a tract back from the sea. The whole of the Flevoland was once covered by the sea. In other parts, the people can only live behind protecting dikes, because the land they live on is below sea level. Planes from all over the world land day after day at Holland's international Schiphol Airport, which lies below sea level. Sometimes the Dutch have deliberately allowed the water back into the country and used it as a military weapon. When the Spaniards were besieging the city of Leyden in 1574, the governor William the Silent ordered the dikes to be pierced and the land flooded. The Spaniards were forced to withdraw. This battle between the Dutch and the Spaniards near Leyden was one stage in the struggle for independence and the creation of Holland, or more correctly the Netherlands, as a unified state. The "first" Netherlands consisted of a large part of Belgium as well as the area covered by the present state. At the beginning of the 16th century Charles V, the German Emperor and King of Spain, had, as overlord of the various earldoms, duchies and bishoprics, united the Netherlands and put them under the rule of his son Philip II. But the staunchly Calvinist Dutch in the north in particular would have no truck with the Catholic Spaniards. They rebelled, and an 80-year-long struggle for freedom ensued. The Westphalian Peace of 1648 ended the eighty-

Sie haben in zähem Kampf dem Meer manche Fläche wieder abgerungen. Das ganze Flevoland war einst vom Meer bedeckt. An anderen Stellen können die Holländer nur im Schutze von Deichen leben, weil ihr Land tiefer liegt als der Meeresspiegel. Täglich landen Flugzeuge aus aller Welt auf Hollands internationalem Flughafen Schiphol bei Amsterdam unter dem Meeresniveau. Manchmal aber haben die Holländer das Wasser als militärische Waffe wieder ins Land zurückgeholt. Als 1574 die Spanier die Stadt Leiden belagerten, ließ der Statthalter Wilhelm der Schweiger die Deiche durchstechen und das Land unter Wasser setzen. Die Spanier mußten abziehen. Dieser Kampf der Holländer gegen die Spanier vor Leiden war eine Etappe des Unabhängigkeitskampfes der Holländer und des Entstehens Hollands, oder sagen wir diesmal besser korrekt, der Niederlande als einem einheitlichen Staat. Diese „ersten" Niederlande umfaßten neben dem Gebiet des heutigen Staates auch den größten Teil Belgiens. Karl V., Anfang des 16. Jahrhunderts deutscher Kaiser und spanischer König, hatte als Herr über die verschiedenen Grafschaften, Herzogtümer und Bistümer die Niederlande zusammengefaßt und die Herrschaft darüber 1556 seinem Sohn Philipp II. übertragen. Doch vor allem die stark calvinistisch geprägten Holländer im Norden des Landes hatten mit den katholischen Spaniern nichts im Sinn. Sie rebellierten, es kam zu einem achtzig Jahre währenden Freiheitskampf. Der Westfälische Friede 1648 been-

dations catastrophiques. La mer a souvent englouti de vastes territoires, perdus pour des centaines d'années. Depuis la nuit des temps, les Hollandais ont tenté de prendre ou reprendre leurs terres à la mer. Autrefois, la province entière de Flevoland était recouverte par la mer. Certains endroits ne sont habitables qu'à l'abri des digues, parce que la terre est sous le niveau de la mer. L'aéroport international de Schiphol près d'Amsterdam où atterrissent des avions du monde entier, est également sous le niveau de la mer. Il est arrivé aussi que les Hollandais se servent de l'eau comme arme de guerre. En 1574, le souverain Guillaume le Taciturne fit percer les digues et inonder la campagne pour chasser les Espagnols qui assiégeaient Leyde. La victoire de Leyde contre les Espagnols est une étape dans la guerre d'Indépendance des Hollandais et la création de la Hollande, ou plus exactement des Pays-Bas, en tant qu'Etat homogène. Ces «premiers» Pays-Bas comprenaient la Hollande actuelle ainsi qu'une grande partie de la Belgique. Au début du 16e siècle, Charles Quint qui était empereur d'Allemagne et roi d'Espagne, avait créé les Pays-Bas à partir des différents comtés, duchés et évêchés sur lesquels il régnait et en avait donné la souveraineté à son fils Philippe II en 1556. Mais les Hollandais calvinistes du nord du pays n'acceptaient pas les Espagnols catholiques. Leur rébellion entraîna 80 ans de guerres qui se terminèrent par le traité de paix de Westphalie en 1648. Les Espagnols conservèrent les Pays-Bas du Sud qui sont

オランダ人は、この海を軍隊兵器として利用し国を取り、返したりもした。１５７４年、スペイン人が、レイデン市を包囲した際、市長のウィルヘルムは、堤防を壊し、国を海面下に沈ませてしまった。スペイン人は撤去せざるを得なかった。レイデンのオランダ人対スペイン人のこの戦いは、オランダ人の独立戦争の始まりでもあり、オランダという国の誕生の始まりでもある。正しくは、統一国家としてのオランダの始まりといったほうがいいだろう。この「最初」のオランダは、現在のオランダ領の他に、ベルギーの大部分も含まれていた。１６世紀の初めにドイツ皇帝でもあり、スペイン王でもあったカール五世は、支配者として、各地にちらばっていた伯爵領、公爵領、教会領等を一緒にした。そして１５５６年に支配権を息子のフィリップ二世に譲った。ところが敬虔なカルビン派の北オランダ人は、カトリック教徒のスペイン人とは、あわなかった。

彼等は反乱を起こし、８０年間にわたる自由戦争が勃発した。この８０年戦争は、１６４８年のウェストファーレン和平条約で終わりを告げた。南オランダ即ち、ベルギーはスペイン領として残り、北オランダはオランダ国として、統一され、オラニエ家が支配者となった。

year war. The southern Netherlands, comprising Belgium, remained under Spanish rule; the northern Netherlands, our destination, gained independence as the United Provinces. The House of Orange took over the governorship.

At the Congress of Vienna both parts of the Netherlands, Holland and Belgium, were then united as the Kingdom of the United Netherlands. William of Orange, the son of the last governor, became King. He is the great-great-great grandfather of the present Queen Beatrix. In 1830, Catholic and partly French-speaking Belgium withdrew from the Netherlands, becoming an independent kingdom. Since then the borders of Holland have remained unchanged.

Living by the water, by the sea, by the rivers and canals made the Dutch a nation of seafarers, navigators and merchants from the beginning. The Dutch navy was at times the largest in the world, and from the East Indian (Indonesian) colonies they brought back hitherto unknown treasures to Europe. In its Golden Age, the 17th century, Amsterdam was the richest merchant city in the world. It is still one of the most beautiful and most visited cities on this earth.

But it is not only the splendid townscapes that bear witness to Holland's former prosperity, in Amsterdam, Haarlem, Delft, Hoorn and the other cities from which the United East India Company operated, the largest trading organization of the then world. The Golden Age of trade and navigation was also a period when art flourished. Rembrandt or Frans Hals are the names

dete diesen achtzigjährigen Krieg. Die südlichen Niederlande, also Belgien, blieben bei Spanien, die nördlichen Niederlande, unser Reiseland, schlossen sich zur Republik der Vereinigten Niederlande zusammen. Das Haus Oranien übernahm die Statthalterschaft.

Der Wiener Kongreß vereinte 1815 wiederum beide Niederlande, Holland und Belgien zum Königreich der Vereinigten Niederlande. König wurde Wilhelm I. von Oranien, der Sohn des letzten Statthalters, der Urururgroßvater der heutigen Königin Beatrix. 1830 trennte sich das rein katholische und zum Teil französischsprachige Belgien von den Niederlanden, wurde ein selbständiges Königreich. Seitdem blieben die Grenzen Hollands unverändert.

Das Leben am Wasser, am Meer, an den Strömen und Kanälen hat die Holländer seit jeher zu Seefahrern, zu Schiffahrts- und Handelsleuten gemacht. Ihre Flotte war zeitweise die größte der Welt, aus ihren ostindischen (indonesischen) Kolonien brachten sie bis dahin unbekannte Kostbarkeiten nach Europa. Amsterdam war im Goldenen Zeitalter, dem 17. Jahrhundert, die reichste Handelsstadt der Welt. Es ist immer noch eine der schönsten und meistbesuchten Städte der Erde.

Doch nicht nur die prächtigen alten Stadtbilder von Amsterdam und Haarlem, Delft, Hoorn und den anderen Städten, von denen aus die Vereinigte Ostindische Kompanie, die größte Handelsgesellschaft der damaligen Welt, tätig war, künden vom einstigen Wohlstand Hollands. Das Goldene Zeitalter des Handels und der Schiffahrt war auch eine Blütezeit der Kunst. Rembrandt

la Belgique actuelle tandis que les Pays-Bas du Nord, la Hollande d'aujourd'hui, devinrent les Provinces-Unies qui passèrent plus tard sous l'autorité de la maison d'Orange.

En 1815, le Congrès de Vienne réunit de nouveau la Hollande et la Belgique, créant le royaume des Pays-Bas dont le souverain était Guillaume I d'Orange, aïeul de Beatrix, la reine actuelle. La Belgique, catholique et en partie de langue française, se détacha des Pays-Bas en 1830 pour devenir un royaume autonome. Les frontières de la Hollande n'ont plus changé depuis cette date.

La vie au bord de la mer, des fleuves et des canaux a fait des Hollandais un peuple de marins et de marchands. A certaines époques, leur flotte était la plus grande du monde. Ils introduisirent en Europe des marchandises précieuses jusqu'alors inconnues, rapportées de leurs colonies de l'Asie du Sud-Est (Indonésie). Au 17e siècle, l'âge d'or de la Hollande, Amsterdam était la ville commerçante la plus riche du monde. Elle est encore une des métropoles les plus belles et les plus visitées du monde.

La prospérité de cette époque se révèle dans les superbes quartiers historiques d'Amsterdam, de Haarlem, de Delft, de Hoorn et des autres villes où la compagnie des Indes Orientales – la principale compagnie de commerce de ce temps – avait des comptoirs. L'âge d'or du commerce et de la navigation fut aussi une période florissante dans le domaine artistique. Citons les célèbres Rembrandt et Frans Hals comme représentants des nombreux peintres dont on peut admi-

１８１４年のウィーン会議ではオランダとベルギーの両国は、再びオランダ王国として統一した。オラニエ家のウィルヘルム一世が王となった。現在のベアトリックス王女の祖、祖、祖父にあたる。１８３０年、生粋のカトリックであり、一部はフランス語圏であるベルギーは、オランダから分かれ、独立王国となった。以来、両国の国境は変わっていない。水、海、河、運河の生活は、オランダ人を船乗りに、海運商人に成らしめた。その海運力が世界一であった時代もある。東インド（インドネシア）植民地から見知らぬ貴重品をヨーロッパに持ち帰った。アムステルダムは、１７世紀に黄金時代をむかえ、世界一裕福な町であった。今でも一番美しい、一番訪問客　の多い処の一つである。

　　　　　　　アムステルダムの壮麗な古い町並みや、ハールレム、デルフト、ホールン、その他の町、当時、世界で一番大きかった東インド会社は、オランダに空前の文化生活を持ち込んだのである。商業や海運の黄金時代は芸術に於いても華やかな時代をもたらしたのである。レンブラントやフランス・ハルス等が画家として有名であり、アムステルダムのリークス博物館、ハーグのマウリテュイス、ハールレムのフランス・ハルス博物館等で彼等の作品を見ることができる。

of just two great painters whose works can be admired in Holland's great museums, such as the Rijksmuseum in Amsterdam, the Mauritshuis in Den Haag or the Frans Hals Museum in Haarlem.

The population of Holland is as varied as the different landscapes of this country, fragmented as it is by the water. The people of Amsterdam are open-minded and cosmopolitan; the villagers in many a small fishing village on the Ijsselmeer withdrawn, protective of their past, preserving old traditions in their communities, their costumes and customs. The Catholic Limburgers are cheerful and merry, the Calvinists in the north strictly puritan. And finally the Frisians on the islands and in the province of Friesland even speak their own language.

The miles and miles of red and yellow tulip fields that stretch out each spring in Noord-Holland contrast with the stern moorlands of Drenthe and Gelderland. And the farming communities in Overijssel, where even today cows are ferried back and forth to their pastures by boat, with the huge greenhouse complexes in West Holland.

The windmills are Holland's archetypal architectural landmarks. The wind blowing off the sea is as constant and reliable as the tides that roll incessantly towards the shore. There are still more than a thousand windmills scattered across the country, some as museum pieces, some still working. They grind grain to flour or draw water from the low-lying polders. They grind the land dry, the saying goes.

oder Frans Hals mögen stellvertretend für die Namen der Maler stehen, deren Werke heute in den großen Museen Hollands zu bewundern sind.

So uneinheitlich wie das vom Wasser zerrissene Land, so uneinheitlich ist auch die Bevölkerung Hollands. Weltoffen, aufgeschlossen sind die Amsterdamer. Eng, bewahrend, am Althergebrachten in Siedlungsformen, Trachten und Bräuchen festhaltend die Menschen in manchen kleinen Fischerdörfern am Ijsselmeer. Eher lebensfroh sind die katholischen Limburger, streng puritanisch die Calvinisten des Nordens. Und die Friesen schließlich auf den Inseln und in der Provinz Friesland sprechen sogar ihre eigene Sprache, das Friesische. Den roten und gelben Tulpenfeldern, die sich im Frühjahr kilometerweit in Noord-Holland dehnen, stehen die ernsten Moor- und Heidelandschaften in Drenthe und Gelderland gegenüber. Und den riesigen Treibhauskulturen im Westen Hollands jene Bauern in Overijssel, die heute noch ihre Kühe mit dem Boot vom Stall zur Weide und wieder zurück bringen. Zum architektonischen Wahrzeichen Hollands schlechthin wurden die Windmühlen. Der Wind, der vom Meer über das Land weht, ist so beständig und zuverlässig wie die Gezeiten, die unablässig gegen das Land rollen. Mehr als tausend Windmühlen stehen heute noch über das Land verstreut, manche als Museumsstücke, manche arbeiten noch. Mahlen Getreide zu Mehl oder schöpfen das Wasser aus tiefer gelegenem Polderland. Sie mahlen das Land trocken, sagt man nicht von ungefähr.

rer les œuvres dans les grands musées de Hollande tels que le Rijksmuseum à Amsterdam, le Mauritshuis à La Haye et le musée Frans Hals à Haarlem.

Le peuple hollandais est aussi peu homogène que son pays fragmenté par les eaux. Les habitants d'Amsterdam sont cosmopolites et ouverts tandis que les habitants de certains villages de pêcheurs de l'Ijsselmeer restent très attachés aux costumes et coutumes anciens. Les Limbourgeois catholiques sont plutôt bons vivants tandis que les Calvinistes du nord restent des puritains. Les habitants des îles de la Frise occidentale et de la Frise parlent même leur propre langue, le frison. Les champs de tulipes jaunes et rouges qui, au printemps, s'étendent sur des kilomètres en Hollande-Septentrionale contrastent avec les paysages sévères de landes et de tourbières des provinces Drenthe et Gueldre. A l'ouest du pays, on pratique des cultures en serre à grande échelle alors que les paysans de la province d'Overijssel transportent encore leurs vaches en barque de l'étable aux pâturages.

Les moulins à vent sont un véritable symbole architectural de la Hollande. Le vent marin qui souffle sur le pays a la même régularité que le flux et le reflux perpétuels des marées. Il existe encore plus de mille moulins en Hollande; certains sont devenus musées, mais beaucoup ont gardé leur fonction d'origine: moudre le grain ou pomper l'eau dans les régions des polders, les terres gagnées sur la mer. Ils moulent une bonne terre bien sèche, dit-on, et c'est vrai.

水によって、国がばらばらに裂かれたように、オランダの国民もまちまちである。アムステルダムの世界に目を向け、オープンな人々もいれば、イーゼルメールの小さな漁村に住む人達のように昔の生活様式を持続し、民族衣装や習慣を保持したいと思っている人達も多い。
カトリックが多いリンブルフ人は、どちらかというと生活をエンジョイする人達、北に住むカルビン派信者は非常に清教徒的である。フリース人は、島でもフリース地方でも、フリース語という独自の言葉を使っている。春には、何キロにも渡って赤や黄色のチューリップ畑が広がる北ホーラント州と対照的に、ドレンテ州やヘルダーラント州では沼地や荒れ野が続く。西オランダには、巨大な温室があり、オーファルライセル州の農家では、今でもボートで牛を牛舎と牧場とを往復している。オランダの建物の象徴は風車である。海から陸へ吹く風は、必ず訪れる干満潮のように永続的に確実に吹く。今でも１０００コ以上の風車がこの国にはある。そのうち、いくつかは博物館となっているが、まだ動いているのもある。穀物を粉にするため、あるいは低地のポルダーランドの水を汲み出すためである。水をひいて、国を乾かすといったのも偶然にではないだろう。

"There is Amsterdam – and the rest of the world," so say the inhabitants of the Dutch capital. As you wander through the old town you quickly come to understand the pride behind this claim. About a thousand bridges link the countless islands in the spider's web of canals that encompass the city centre in a network of semi-circles.

„Es gibt Amsterdam – und den Rest der Welt", sagen die Bewohner der holländischen Hauptstadt. Bei einem Bummel durch die Altstadt wird man den Stolz, der aus diesem Satz spricht, schnell verstehen. Rund tausend Brücken verbinden die unzähligen Inseln im spinnwebartigen Netz der Grachten und Kanäle, die sich in konzentrischen Halbkreisen um den alten Kern schmiegen.

« Il y a Amsterdam ... et le reste du monde », affirment les habitants de la capitale néerlandaise. On comprend très vite cette phrase fière en se promenant dans la vieille-ville d'Amsterdam. Quelque mille ponts réunissent les innombrables îlots dans le réseau de canaux en toile d'araignée qui entoure le cœur de la cité en demi-cercles concentriques.

「まずアムステルダム － そして残りの世界がある。」旧市街を散策してみると この文章の意味がすぐわかる。そこには旧市街を中心に半月状に運河が流れ、約１０００カ所に網の目のように橋がかけられ、数え切れない程の島々を結んでる。市の中心まで続くこの水路に沿って古い家並が建ち並び、このファサードは７００年の市の歴史を物語っているのでる。

The old houses line up proudly along the waterways that criss-cross the city, 700 years of history reflected in their facades. – At the junction of the river Amstel and the Ij, a branch of the Ijsselmeer, a small 13th century fishing village grew into an international metropolis. As the ground in the Amstel valley was marshy, the stone houses had to be built on thousands and thousands of piles.

Entlang der Wasserstraßen, die die Stadt bis ins Herz durchziehen reihen sich die alten Häuser aneinander, in deren Fassaden sich 700 Jahre Stadtgeschichte spiegeln. – An der Mündung der Amstel in das Ij am Ausfluß aus dem Ijsselmeer entwickelte sich seit dem 13. Jahrhundert das kleine Fischerdorf zur Weltstadt.

Les quais sont bordés d'admirables maisons anciennes dont les façades racontent 700 ans d'histoire. Situé à l'embouchure de l'Amstel et de l'Ij, au bout de l'Ijsselmeer (Lac d'Yssel), l'ancien village de pêcheurs s'est développé en une métropole depuis le 13e siècle. Le bas-fond de l'Amstel étant marécageux, les maisons durent être érigées sur des dizaines de milliers de pilotis.

アムステル川の河口、アイセルメールからアイ川が流れ出る処で、１３世紀には小さな漁村であった処が世界都市に発展したのである。アムステル川低地は湿地地帯であったため、何千本という柱を打ち込んで石造りの家を建てなければならなかった。

By the 17th century Amsterdam had become the richest and most powerful trading city in Europe. Today it is one of the most frequently visited cities in the world. There is not much room for cars in the narrow streets along the canals. Bicycles, or fiets, are the characteristic mode of transport. And of course boats.

Weil der Boden in der Amstelniederung morastig war, mußten die steinernen Häuser auf zehntausenden von Pfählen errichtet werden. Im 17. Jahrhundert wurde Amsterdam die reichste und mächtigste Handelsstadt Europas. Heute ist die holländische Hauptstadt eine der meistbesuchten Städte der Welt. Auf den schmalen Straßen entlang der Grachten ist nicht viel Platz für Autos.

Amsterdam était la ville de commerce la plus riche et la plus puissante d'Europe au 17e siècle. Aujourd'hui, la capitale hollandaise est une des villes les plus visitées du monde. Les voitures n'ont guère de place sur les quais étroits qui longent les canaux. La bicyclette est le moyen de transport le plus usité, ainsi que le bateau.

１７世紀には、アムステルダムはヨーロッパ一裕福で権力的な商業都市となった。今日では、このオランダの首都は、世界で一番訪問客の多い都市の一つである。運河沿いの道路は狭く、車は通りにくい。自転車が典型的なアムステル人の交通機関である。そして、もちろんボートもである。

Excursion boats and water taxis criss-cross the city, passing through locks and under drawbridges. Often they travel at night, when thousands of lights cast a magic spell over the city. Artists have always felt at home in Amsterdam. World-famous museums like the Rijksmuseum have made Amsterdam an international art centre as well as a centre of the art and antiques trade.

Ausflugsboote und Wassertaxis fahren kreuz und quer durch die Stadt, durch Schleusen und unter Zugbrücken hindurch. Oft fahren sie auch noch am Abend wenn tausende von Lichtern die Stadt verzaubern. Künstler haben sich in Amsterdam immer wohlgefühlt. Weltberühmte Museen, wie das Rijksmuseum, machen Amsterdam zur internationalen Kunststadt.

Une expérience inoubliable est de visiter la ville illuminée le soir à bord d'un bateau de croisière. Les artistes ont toujours apprécié Amsterdam qui est une ville d'art internationale grâce à des musées mondialement connus tels que le Rijksmuseum et un marché florissant d'antiquités et d'art.

観光用ボートや、水上タクシーが右往左往と町を、水門を、鉄道橋の下を走っている。それらは町の明りがきれいな夜も走っている。
芸術家にとってもアムステルダムはいい町であった。リークス博物館のような世界的に有名な博物館もあり、国際芸術都市であり、芸術と古物商の町でもある。

Beautiful old artefacts, the old Dutch way of life and old buildings can of course also be found in Holland's open-air museums. One such museum village is the Zaanse Schans north of Amsterdam. The old villages in this historic region served as a model. The windmills are reflected in the water, this all-pervading element that dominates the land. And also the little old town of Alkmaar with its drawbridges.

ZAANSE SCHANS   ALKMAAR

Schöne alte Dinge, Formen alter holländischer Lebensart und alte Gebäude findet man natürlich auch in den Freilichtmuseen des Landes. Ein solches Museumsdorf ist die Zaanse Schans nördlich von Amsterdam. Es ist den alten Dörfern dieser historischen Landschaft nachgebaut. Die Windmühlen spiegeln sich im Wasser, das alles beherrschend das Land durchdringt. Auch die kleine, alte Stadt Alkmaar mit ihren Zugbrücken.

ZAANSE SCHANS   ALKMAAR

On découvre également l'architecture et les traditions hollandaises anciennes dans les musées de plein air du pays. Celui de Zaanse Schans, au nord d'Amsterdam, est un village historiquement reconstitué selon les anciens villages de la région. Les moulins se reflètent dans l'eau qui domine le paysage. Elle est aussi omniprésente dans la petite ville d'Alkmaar aux nombreux ponts mobiles.

ザーンセ・　スカンスとアルクマール

きれいで古い物、古いオランダの生活様式、古い建物等は、国の野外博物館で見られる。この博物館村がアムステルダムの北にあるザーンス・スカンスである。古い村にこの歴史的な物を増築したのである。風車が水に映る様子はこの土地ならである。この小さな町、アルクマールには、はね橋もある。

Alkmaar, a town situated close to the resorts of northern Holland, captivates its visitors with its old-world atmosphere. Fine old burgher houses dating from the 16th – 18th century remind us that this town on the North Holland Canal was once an important trading town. In 1528 the burghers of Alkmaar turned the church of the Holy Ghost hospital into a weighbridge.

Alkmaar, nahe den nordholländischen Küstenbadeorten bezaubert schon durch sein altertümliches Stadtbild. Zahlreiche schöne Bürgerhäuser aus dem 16.–18. Jahrhundert erinnern daran, daß die Stadt am Nordhollandkanal einmal eine wichtige Handelsstadt war. 1582 bauten die Bürger von Alkmaar die Kirche des Heiliggeistspitals um und machten eine Waage daraus.

Alkmaar, située près des stations balnéaires de la côte nord hollandaise, ravit d'abord par sa physionomie ancienne. De nombreuses belles maisons patriciennes construites entre les 16e et 18e siècles rappellent que la localité sur les bords du canal de la Hollande du Nord fut une ville de commerce importante. Aujourd'hui, on pèse les fromages dans l'église construite par les habitants en 1582.

北オランダの海水浴場の近くのアルクメールは昔ながらの町の景観が美しい。16世紀から18世紀の市民の住宅が沢山まだ残っており、かつては北オランダ運河沿いの重要な商業都市であったことが伺える。

Every Friday morning from April to October the big colourful cheese market takes place on the square outside, drawing onlookers from far and wide. The whole area is then covered with cartwheel-sized cheeses and countless big balls of cheese. Porters dressed in white smocks with brightly coloured guild hats and sashes come running up, bringing the cheeses on strange-looking stretchers to be weighed.

Auf dem Waagplatz vor dieser Waage findet von April bis Oktober an jedem Freitagmorgen der große, bunte Käsemarkt statt, der Schaulustige von karrenradgroßen Käselaibern und unzähligen dicken Käsekugeln. Dieser Käse wird von Trägern in weißen Kitteln, mit bunten Zunfthüten und -schärpen auf eigenartigen Tragen im Laufschritt zur Waage gebracht und dann verladen.

D'avril à octobre, le grand marché aux fromages qui se tient sur la Waagplatz chaque vendredi matin attire un nombreux public. La place est recouverte de fromages grands comme des roues de charrettes et d'une montagne de boules de fromages. Des hommes en blouse blanche, portant les écharpes et les chapeaux pittoresques de leur corporation transportent leurs charges jusqu'à la balance.

１５８２年にはアルクメールの住民は聖霊病院の教会を計量所に建て替えてしまった。この計量所のある計量所広場では、４月から１０月迄、毎週金曜日の朝、大きなにぎやかなチーズ市が開かれ、遠方からも見物人が沢山やって来る。

It is not as easy as it looks to get the skillfully piled cheeses to the weighing place both quickly and safely, and then on to the waiting vehicles. Clogs are as essential a part of Holland's image as cheese is. They are sold in the markets, as here in Alkmaar, and still worn in everyday life.

Es ist gar nicht so einfach, die Last mit den geschickt aufgeschichteten Kugeln rasch und dennoch sicher zur Waage und dann weiter zum Transportfahrzeug zu schaffen. Untrennbar wie der Käse gehören auch die Holzschuhe zum Bild Hollands. Auf den Märkten, wie hier in Alkmaar, werden die Klompen verkauft und im Alltagsleben noch immer getragen.

Ce n'est pas une tâche facile que d'effectuer le trajet au pas de course avec les fromages empilés sur des sortes des brancards. Les sabots en bois font autant partie de l'image de la Hollande que les fromages. Ils sont vendus sur les marchés, comme ici à Alkmaar, et sont encore portés dans la vie quotidienne.

全広場が荷車の車輪程もあるチーズの塊や、分厚いチーズボールで埋め尽くされる。このチーずを、白い作業着に色々な職業組合の帽子をかぶった作業員が走りながら秤まで運び、秤に乗せる。この重さの丸チーズを速く、落とさず秤まで運び、それをまた運搬車迄持っていくのはそう簡単な事ではない。

Haarlem, only a few kilometres from the North Sea, is considered the most elegant town in Holland. In the 11th to 13th century the town on the Spaarne was the seat of the Duke of Holland. The mighty tower of the church of St. Bavo still towers above Haarlem today. Mozart gave a concert at the organ of this church at the age of nine.

Als vornehmste Stadt Hollands gilt Haarlem, nur wenige Kilometer von der Nordsee entfernt. Im 11. bis 13. Jahrhundert war die Stadt am Spaarne Residenz der Grafen von Holland. Der mächtige Turm der St.-Bavokirche überragt Haarlem heute noch. An der Orgel dieser Kirche hat W. A. Mozart im Alter von neun Jahren bereits ein Konzert gegeben.

Haarlem qui n'est située qu'à quelques kilomètres de la Mer du Nord est la ville la plus élégante des Pays-Bas. Elle fut la résidence des comtes de Hollande du 11e au 13e siècles. Les tours majestueuses de l'église St. Bavo dominent encore la physionomie de la ville. Mozart y donna un concert d'orgues à l'âge de neuf ans.

オランダで一番上品な町といわれるハーレムは、北海から数キロしか離れていない。１１世紀から１３世紀には、スパールネ川の辺りのこの町にオランダの伯爵の城があった。
聖バボー教会の巨大な塔がハーレムに今もそびえたっている。モーツァルトは９歳の時に、この教会でオルガンコンサートを行っている。１７世紀の初めに建てられた肉用ホールは、

Zandvoort, situated just outside Haarlem, has grown into the most well-known seaside resort in Holland. With its broad beach of fine sand, a busy boulevard and a lively night-life Zandvoort draws people like a magnet from all along the coast. In June and September there is international motor racing on the racing circuit.

Vor den Toren Haarlems entwickelt sich Zandvoort zum bekanntesten Badeort Nord-Hollands. Mit seinem breiten, feinsandigen Strand, einem belebten Boulevard und einem lebhaften Nachtleben ist Zandvoort ein besonderer Magnet an der Küste. Im Juni und September gibt es auf der Rennstrecke von Zandvoort internationale Autorennen.

Zandvoort, située aux portes de Haarlem, est devenue la station balnéaire la plus réputée de la Hollande-Septentrionale. Elle attire un large public grâce à sa vaste plage de sable fin, son atmosphère animée et sa vie nocturne. Chaque année, en juin et septembre, le circuit de Zandvoort est la scène de courses automobiles internationales.

ハーレムのすぐ隣のザントフォールトは、北オランダで一番有名な海水浴場として発展してきた。幅広い、細かい砂の浜辺、活気ある大通り、にぎやかな夜の町等が特に人をこの町に引きつける。6月と9月には、ここで国際自動車レースも開かれる。

Holland is known as a flower-growing country all over the world. At the beginning of May the De Keukenhof castle park near Lisse seems to literally exlode in a spectacular show of flowers. A sea of narcissi, tulip and hyacinth blooms makes Keukenhof one of the most beautiful gardens in the world. Holland's career as a flower-growing country began when the first tulip bulbs were secretly smuggled out of

In aller Welt ist Holland als Blumenland bekannt. Anfang Mai scheint der Park des Schlosses De Keukenhof bei Lisse geradezu in einer einzigartigen Blumenpracht zu explodieren. Dann machen hier unzählige Narzissen-, Tulpen und Hyazinthenblüten Keukenhof zu einer der schönsten Gartenanlagen der Welt. Angefangen hat Hollands Karriere als Blumenland, als um 1600 die ersten Tulpenzwiebeln heimlich aus

La Hollande est connue dans le monde entier comme le pays des fleurs. Le parc du château de Keukenhof près de Lisse présente une magnificence fleurie unique au début du mois de mai. Des multitudes de narcisses, hyacinthes et tulipes le transforment en un des plus beaux jardins du monde. C'est vers 1600 que les premiers oignons de tulipes venant de Turquie, ont été introduits en secret en Hollande.

オランダは全世界に花の国として知られている。5月初め、リッセの近くのキューケンホーフ城公園は花が咲き乱れる。すいせん、チューリップ、ヒアシンス等々。キューケンホーフはこの時期、世界で一番美しい公園の一つと化するのである。

Turkey around 1600 and brought to Holland, and soon business with the "Bloembollen", the bulbs, developed into a veritable flower rush. The tulip fields in bloom turn the Bloembollen area in northern Holland into an overwhelming sea of colour. The bulbs produced here are an important export article for Holland.

der Türkei nach Holland geschafft wurden und alsbald das Geschäft mit den „Bloembollen", den Blumenzwiebeln, in einen regelrechten Boom ausartete. Die Blüte der Tulpenfelder im holländischen Blumenzwiebelgebiet ist ein einziger Farbenrausch. Die hier gewonnenen Blumenzwiebeln sind ein wichtiger Exportartikel des Landes.

Le commerce avec les fleurs connut bientôt un essor immense. La symphonie de couleurs glorieuses des champs de tulipes est la marque de la Hollande-Septentrionale. Les oignons cultivés sont un article d'exportation majeur du pays.

花の国としてのオランダの始まりは、16世紀にチューリップの球根をトルコからオランダへ密かに持ち帰ったことから始まる。そして、またたくうちに熱狂的な「花」ブームを巻き起こし、北ホーラントの花畑はチューリップ畑になっていった。ここで作られる花の球根はこの国の重要な輸出製品である。

It isn't far from Noordwijk to Leyden, Holland's city of scholarship. This, the first university of the present-day Netherlands, was founded as early as 1575. It has remained a stronghold of Dutch scholarship till today, famous above all for its medical faculty. At the time, the inhabitants of Leyden are said to have opted for the founding of a university rather than a large tax exemption.

Es ist nicht weit von Noordwijk nach Leiden, Hollands Gelehrtenstadt. Schon 1575 wurde in Leiden die erste Universität der heutigen Niederlande gegründet. Sie ist bis heute ein Hort holländischer Gelehrsamkeit, berühmt vor allem durch ihre medizinische Fakultät. Angeblich sollen die Leidener damals die Universitätsgründung einer großen Steuerfreiheit vorgezogen haben.

La ville universitaire de Leyde n'est qu'à quelques pas de Noordwijk. La première université des Pays-Bas actuels y fut fondée dès 1575. Elle est restée le haut-lieu de l'enseignement en Hollande, réputée notamment pour sa faculté de médecine. A l'époque, ses habitants auraient préféré la création d'une université à une importante exonération fiscale.

ノールドワイクから程遠くないところに、オランダの学問の町といわれるレイデンがある。既に１５７５年には今日のオランダの最初の大学が創立された。この大学は今もなお権威ある大学であり、特に医学部が有名である。この大学の創立でレイデン人はかなりの額が無税になったということである。

The waters of the Old Rhine pass through the town like a series of canals and give visitors the chance to explore the city by boat. Leyden's landmarks are the Hofjes, thirty old almshouses, built mostly in the style of the 16th – 17th century.

Das Wasser des Alten Rheins durchzieht kanalartig die Stadt und gibt die Möglichkeit, sie an Bord von Ausflugsbooten kennenzulernen. Typisch für Leiden sind die Hofjes, dreißig meist im Stil des 16. und 17. Jahrhunderts gebaute Altersheime von jeweils 10–30 Häusern.

On peut visiter la ville à bord de bateaux qui naviguent sur les canaux où coule l'eau du Vieux-Rhin. La physionomie de Leyde est marquée par les trente «Hofjes», des hospices construits aux 16e et 17e siècles, comprenant chacun de 10 à 30 maisons.

旧ライン川が運河の様に町中を流れており、観光用ボートで町を観光することも可能。レイデンで典型的なものは、17世紀から17世紀の様式で建てられそれぞれ10軒から30軒の家が連なるホーフィエス　30である。

The sea is never very far away in Holland, and with it the wind that blows off it. That so quintessentially Dutch building, the windmill, many of which are still standing, most clearly bears witness to this fact. In Leidschendam between Leyden and Den Haag, you can still see some of them, stretching their sails up into the sky.

Das Meer ist überall nahe in Holland und damit auch der Wind, der vom Wasser zum Land weht. Unübersehbare Zeugen dafür sind die vielen Windmühlen, die es heute noch in Holland gibt. Auch in Leidschendam zwischen Leiden und Den Haag recken noch einige dieser typisch holländischen Bauwerke ihre Flügel in den hohen Himmel.

La mer est omniprésente en Hollande et elle apporte le vent qui souffle partout sur le pays. Son énergie a été et est encore capturée par les multiples moulins, symboles de la Hollande. A Leidschendam, située entre Leyde et la Haye, on peut admirer plusieurs moulins à vent qui dressent leurs ailes vers le ciel.

オランダでは至る所海に近い。ということは、風が吹く。風は海から陸にふく。その証拠に、今でもオランダにはたくさんの風車がある。レイデンとハーグの中間にあるレイドスヘンダムにもこの典型的なオランダの建築物が、その羽を空に向けている

Just outside the capital city of Den Haag, lies Scheveningen, the largest seaside resort in Holland, stretching out along the shore. Scheveningen pier extends 400 metres out into the sea. Facing it is the monumental kurhaus, built by German architects in 1884 as an extravagant beach palace.

Vor den Toren der holländischen Residenzstadt Den Haag dehnt sich Scheveningen als größtes Seebad Hollands. 400 Meter weit ragt der Pier von Scheveningen ins Meer hinaus. Ihm gegenüber liegt das monumentale, 1884, von deutschen Architekten als aufwendiger Strandpalast gebaute Kurhaus. Der Badeort Scheveningen ist auch noch ein wichtiger Hafen.

La plus grande station balnéaire de Hollande s'étend aux portes de La Haye (Den Haag). La jetée de Scheveningen s'avance à 400 mètres dans la mer. Juste en face, on peut admirer l'édifice monumental qui abrite les thermes, construit en 1884 par des architectes allemands. Scheveningen est également un port important.

オランダの王室の町ハーグの玄関口にあるスヘベニンヘンはオランダで一番大きい海岸である。400メートルにわたって、スヘベニンヘンの桟橋が海に突き出ている。その反対側には1884年に海岸宮殿としてドイツの設計者によって造られたクアハウスがある。海水浴場スヘベニンヘンはまた重要な港でもある。

In Madurodam on the outskirts of Den Haag you can see Holland in miniature. Houses and castles, windmills, canals, ships and planes, everything that is well-known and typical has been reproduced here on a scale of 1 to 25. On summer evenings there are son et lumière performances called "Moonlight Miracle".

Holland en miniature kann man am Stadtrand von Den Haag in Madurodam erleben. Häuser und Schlösser, Windmühlen, Grachten, Schiffe und Züge, alles, was bekannt und typisch ist in Holland wurde hier originalgetreu im Maßstab 1 : 25 aufgebaut. An Sommerabenden gibt es die Klang- und Lichteffekte „Moonlight Miracle".

On peut voir la Hollande en miniature à Madurodam en banlieue de La Haye dont le nom hollandais officiel est 's Gravenhage. Maisons, châteaux, moulins, canaux, bateaux et trains, tout ce qui est connu et typique en Hollande est reproduit fidèlement à une échelle de 1 : 25. Le spectacle de sons et lumières «Moonlight miracle» agrémente les soirées d'été.

オランダのミニアチュアがハーグの郊外のマドローダムで見られる。ここには家、城、風車、運河、船、列車等、オランダでよく知られ、典型的と思われるもの全てがオリジナルと同じに、1：25で造られている。夏の夜にはサウンドとライト・ショー「ムーンライト・ミラクル」が見られる。

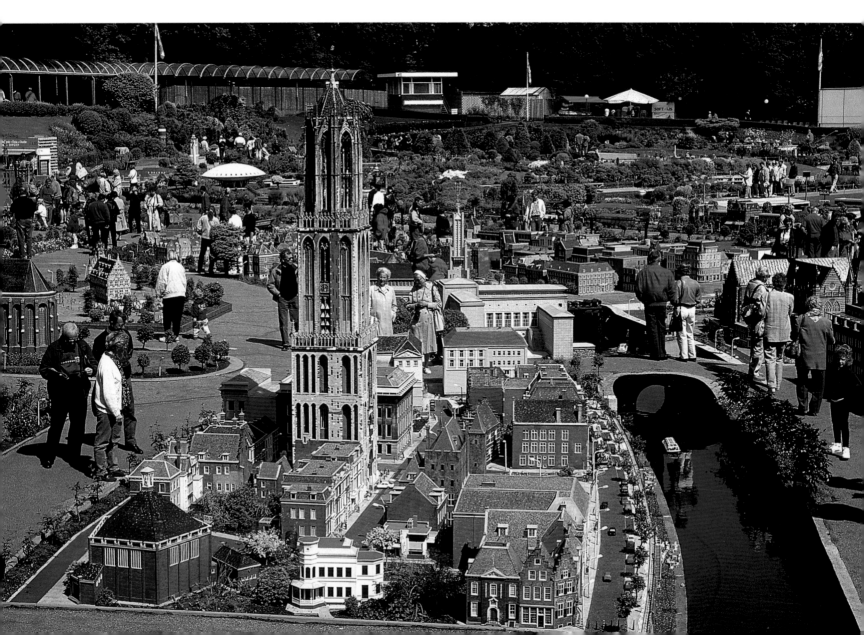

The Dutch seat of government and royal residence, whose correct name is 's-Gravenhage, grew up round a hunting seat that was built in 1284. Today the centre of political life in Holland is a city characterised by modern high-rise buildings. But Den Haag also boasts a whole range of fine buildings and picturesque corners that have been preserved, too.

Die holländische Regierungsstadt und königliche Residenz, die mit korrektem Namen 's-Gravenhage heißt, entwickelte sich um ein 1284 errichtetes Jagdschloß. Heute ist das Zentrum des politischen Lebens Hollands eine Großstadt, die von modernen Hochhäusern geprägt wird. Daneben aber hat sich Den Haag noch eine Fülle schöner Gebäude und malerischer Winkel erhalten.

La Haye, siège du gouvernement et résidence royale, s'est développée à partir d'un château de chasse érigé en 1284. Le centre de la politique néerlandaise est aujourd'hui une métropole moderne qui a cependant conservé un grand nombre de belles constructions anciennes et des coins pittoresques.

オランダの行政首都、王室の城のある町、デン・ ハーグは、正式にはグラーヘンハーヘといい、1284年に建造された狩猟のための城から発展してきたものである。今日では、この政治の中心地は近代的なビルが建ち並ぶ大都市である。

The expanse of water known as the Hofvijvers, the court pond, is one of the nicest parts of the city. In its waters you can see the Binnen and Buitenhof reflected, a group of buildings some of which go back to the hunting seat times of the Duke of Holland. Some of the buildings are where the two chambers of the Dutch parliament reside, some are occupied by the government.

Zu den schönsten Partien der Stadt zählt die Wasserfläche des Hofvijvers (Parlamentsgebäude). In ihm spiegeln sich die Gebäude des Binnen- und Buitenhofes, einer Gruppe von Bauten, die zum Teil noch auf das Jagdschloß der Grafen von Holland zurückgehen. In einigen der Gebäude residieren die beiden Kammern des holländischen Parlamentes, in anderen die Regierung.

Un des plus jolis endroits de la ville est le plan d'eau du «Hofvijvers» dans lequel se reflètent les édifices du Binnenhof et Buitenhof, un groupe de bâtiments qui appartenaient en partie au château de chasse des comtes de Hollande. Le complexe abrite les deux Courts du Parlement néerlandais, le Gouvernement ainsi que le célèbre musée dit Mauruitshuis.

しかしそれと並んで　ハーグには沢山の美しい建物や絵に描いたような一角もある。最も美しいのは、ホーフ－ヴィーヴァー、ホーフヴィアーの水面である。その水面に一部はまだオランダの伯爵の狩猟のための城の建造物が反映して見える。

The Mauritshuis, one of the outstanding museums in the world, is part of this complex. Among the various palaces to be found in Den Haag is the Paleis Noordeinde, reserved today for Queen Beatrix and her family. The palace gardens, however, are open to everybody.

Auch das Mauritshuis, eines der bedeutendsten Museen der Welt, gehört zu diesem Komplex. Unter den verschiedenen Palästen, die in Den Haag zu finden sind ist das Paleis Noordeinde heute für Königin Beatrix und ihre Familie reserviert. Im Palastgarten allerdings darf jeder spazieren gehen.

Parmi les divers palais de la ville, le palais Noordeinde est une résidence privée de la famille royale, mais ses jardins sont ouverts au public.

この建物の幾つかはオランダ議会の両院の建物として使っているし、他の建物は内閣が使用している。又、世界で最も重要な博物館の一つであるマウリッツハイスもこの一角にある。ハーグにある沢山の城の内、ノールドエイネ城に、ベアトリック王女とその家族が住んでいる。しかし、城の庭には誰でも入る事ができる。

Delft, on the way from Den Haag to Rotterdam, had its first Golden Age in medieval times, thanks to its linen-weaving. The town is criss-crossed by canals, the marketplace is considered the finest in South Holland. This is where the Gothic Nieuwe Kerk stands, which contains the crypt of the House of Orange. And it is also where the so-called father of the fatherland, William the Silent is buried.

Zwischen Den Haag und Rotterdam liegt das Städtchen Delft. Grachten und Kanäle durchziehen die Stadt, die im späten Mittelalter dank ihrer Tuchfabriken ein erstes goldenes Zeitalter erlebte. Der Marktplatz von Delft gilt als der schönste Süd-Hollands. An ihm steht die gotische Nieuwe Kerk mit der Gruft des Hauses Oranien. Hier ist auch der als Vater des Vaterlandes bezeichnete Willem der Schweiger begraben.

Delft est située sur la route qui conduit de La Haye à Rotterdam. Un réseau de canaux quadrille la petite ville qui a connu son apogée à la fin du moyen âge grâce à son industrie drapière. L'église gothique Nieuwe Kerk qui se dresse sur la magnifique place du Marché, abrite le tombeau de la famille d'Orange-Nassau. C'est ici qu'est enterré Guillaume le Taciturne, considéré comme le père de la patrie.

ハーグとロッテルダムの間に小さな町デルフトがある。運河が町の中を流れている。中世の後期に布工場があったため、黄金時代を迎える。デルフトの市場広場は南ホーランド州で一番美しいとされている。この広場にはオラニエ家の納骨室のある新教会がある。ここには祖国の父といわれるウィレム皇が埋葬されている。

Delft became world-famous through its blue-painted pottery and porcelain. The ships of the United East India Company, whose office was in Delfshaven, brought Chinese porcelain back from the Far East, which potters and porcelain painters in Delft then used as a model.

Weltberühmt wurde Delft durch seine blau bemalten Kacheln. Die Schiffe der Vereinigten Ostindischen Kompanie, deren Büro sich in Delfshaven befand, brachten chinesisches Porzellan aus dem Fernen Osten mit, das den Delfter Töpfern und Porzellanmalern als Vorbild diente.

La ville est mondialement réputée pour ses faïences peintes en bleu. Les navires de la compagnie des Indes Orientales, dont le siège était dans le port de Delft, ont rapporté les porcelaines chinoises de l'Asie lointaine qui ont inspiré les potiers et peintres de porcelaine de Delft.

世界的に有名な物としてブルーで描かれたタイルがある。
デルフスハーフェンに事務所があった統一東インド会社の船がアジアから中国の磁器を持ち帰り、磁器を作る人や、磁器に絵を描く人達の手本になった。

The end of the Nieuwe Waterweg (1866-1872), where the waters of the Rhine and the Maas flow into the North Sea, is where Hoek van Holland, today part of Rotterdam, grew into Holland's most important port for ferry services to and from England. Countless industrial plants line the waterway between the two towns.

Wo der 1866 bis 1872 geschaffene Nieuwe Waterweg das Wasser von Rhein und Maas zur Nordsee fließen läßt entwickelte sich Hoek van Holland zum wichtigsten Fährhafen Hollands im Verkehr mit England. Heute gehört Hoek van Holland, das auch als Seebad besucht wird zu Rotterdam. Unzählige Industrieanlagen säumen den Wasserweg zwischen den beiden Städten.

Hœk van Holland est le premier port de Hollande pour le trafic des voyageurs vers l'Angleterre. La ville est située sur le canal Nieuwe Waterweg, construit de 1866 à 1872, qui emporte les eaux du Rhin et de la Meuse vers la mer du Nord. Elle est également une station balnéaire et fait partie de Rotterdam. De nombreuses industries bordent la partie du canal entre les deux villes.

１８６６年から１８７２年にかけて造られた新水路でライン川やマース川が北海に流れ込む処にあるヘーク・ファンホランドは、イギリスとの交通に重要なフェリーポートとして発展してきた。今日では、海水浴客も来るこの町はロッテルダムに属している。この２都市の間には、多くの工業プラントがある。

The port of Rotterdam is the largest in the world in terms of the amount of goods that are handled. Its importance is chiefly due to its function as a link between maritime shipping and vessels transporting mass-produced goods down the Rhine on inland shipping routes through Germany.

Rotterdams Hafen gilt vom Güterumschlag her als der größte der Welt. Seine Bedeutung liegt vor allem in seiner Umschlagfunktion zwischen der Hochseeschiffahrt, vor allem für Massengüter und der Binnenschiffahrt über den Rhein und in das deutsche Binnenschifffahrtskanalnetz.

Rotterdam est le plus grand port au monde pour le trafic des marchandises, notamment pour le transbordement des matières premières entre les navires océaniques et la navigation fluviale sur le Rhin et sur tout le réseau de canaux allemand.

ロッテルダム港は貨物の積み替えからすると世界で一番大きい。特に海洋船で、大量のばら荷を積んで来た船は、ここで荷をライン川やドイツ内陸水路網を走る内陸船に積み替えられる。こうした積み替え機能がこの港の特に重要なものである。ロッテルダムの港観光船に乗ってみるのも、オランダ旅行のとてもいい体験になるだろう。

A boat trip round Rotterdam harbour is one of the most impressive and lasting memories of a tour of Holland. Rotterdam was largely destroyed in the Second World War. The gate to Europe, as people like to call the city, was rebuilt and is now characterised by modern architecture. The avant-garde architecture by the Oude Haven is as much part of this as are the skyscrapers in the city centre.

Eine Hafenrundfahrt in Rotterdam gehört zu den besonders eindrucksvollen Erlebnissen einer Hollandreise. Im 2. Weltkrieg wurde Rotterdam weitgehend zerstört. Inzwischen ist das Tor zu Europa, wie man die Stadt nennt, wieder aufgebaut und durch moderne Architektur geprägt. Dazu gehört die avantgardistische Kubusarchitektur am Oude Haven ebenso wie die Wolkenkratzer im Stadtzentrum.

La visite des installations portuaires devrait absolument faire partie d'un voyage en Hollande. Gravement endommagée durant la seconde guerre mondiale, la «Porte sur l'Europe», ainsi qu'on nomme Rotterdam, présente aujourd'hui une physionomie très moderne dont témoignent notamment l'architecture avant-gardiste au Oude Haven et les gratte-ciel du centre ville.

第2次世界大戦でロッテルダムはかなり破壊された。ヨーロッパへの門と呼ばれるこの町も今では再建され、近代建築物が建ち並ぶ。オーデ・ハーフェンには前衛立方体建築が、町の中心には超高層ビルが見られる。

Rotterdam is not only the largest port of the world, in which annually million tons are turned over by goods. It is with annually more than 300 meetings culture capital, which find not only in the arts centers instead of, but also in the free one. Beyond that there is large Festivals in the summer months like the Dunya Festival, the Solero Sommerkarneval and the FFWD Heineken Danceparade.

Rotterdam ist nicht nur der größte Hafen der Welt, in dem jährlich Millionen Tonnen von Gütern umgeschlagen werden. Sie ist mit jährlich mehr als 300 Veranstaltungen Kulturhauptstadt, die nicht nur in den Kunsthallen statt finden, sondern auch im Freien. Darüber hinaus gibt es in den Sommermonaten große Festivals wie das Dunya Festival, den Solero Sommerkarneval und die FFWD Heineken Danceparade.

Rotterdam est non seulement le plus grand port du monde, en lequel annuellement million de tonnes sont retournées par des marchandises. Il est avec le capital de culture d'annuellement plus de 300 réunions, au lieu des lesquels trouvez non seulement aux centres d'arts, mais également dans les libres. Au delà de cela il y a de grands festivals en mois d'été comme le festival de Dunya, le Solero Sommerkarneval et le FFWD Heineken Danceparade.

ロッテルダムは毎年何百万トンもの貨物が入れ換わる、世界最大の港であるばかりではなく、毎年三百件以上もの催し物が、美術館のみならず屋外にても催される文化首都でもあります。夏はそれに加えてドゥニヤフェスティバル (Dunya Festival)、ソレロの夏カーニバル (Solero Sommerkarneval)、さらにハイネケン FFWD ダンスパレード (FFWD Heineken Danceparade)といった大規模なフェスティバルが有ります。

Gouda, situated between Rotterdam and Utrecht, was an important trading centre as early as the 15th century. Today it is known mainly for its cheese market, which takes place every Thursday in summer on the triangular marketplace. In the middle, the Gothic town hall rises up like a stone reliquary. It is the oldest town hall in Holland, dating back to 1450.

Schon im 15. Jahrhundert war Gouda, zwischen Rotterdam und Utrecht gelegen, ein wichtiges Handelszentrum. Heute ist es vor allem berühmt durch seinen Käsemarkt, der im Sommer jeden Donnerstag auf dem dreieckigen Marktplatz stattfindet. Mitten auf diesem Platz erhebt sich wie ein steinerner Reliquienschrein das gotische Rathaus von 1450 als ältestes in ganz Holland.

Gouda qui s'étend entre Rotterdam et Utrecht, était déjà un centre de commerce important au 15e siècle. Aujourd'hui, la ville est surtout réputée pour son marché au fromage qui a lieu tous les jeudis en été sur la place du Marché. L'hôtel de ville gothique de 1450 se dresse au centre de la place triangulaire. Ressemblant à un reliquaire en pierre, il est le plus ancien hôtel de ville du pays.

ロッテルダムとユトレヒトの間にあるハウダは、すでに13世紀には重要な商業の中心であった。今日では、夏の毎週木曜日に三角形の市場広場で行われるチーズ市で有名。この広場の真ん中に、1450年に建てられたオランダで一番古いゴチック式市庁舎が石の聖記念堂のように建っている。

Nineteen old windmills are still to be seen along the Lek, the northern of the two big branches of the Dutch Rhine near Rotterdam. These were not mills for grinding corn. As so often in Holland, they were polder mills, designed to drive big pumps that were used for draining the land.

Neunzehn alte Windmühlen sind am Lek, dem nördlichen der beiden großen Rheinarme in Holland nahe Rotterdam noch zu sehen. Diese Mühlen waren keine Mahlmühlen. Es waren – wie so oft in Holland – Poldermühlen, dazu bestimmt mit Windkraft große Schöpfpumpen zu bedienen, mit denen das Land entwässert werden konnte.

Dix-neuf vieux moulins bordent le Lek, ainsi que s'appelle la partie d'un des deux grands bras du Rhin près de Rotterdam. Ces moulins ne servaient pas à moudre le grain. Comme bien d'autres en Hollande, ils étaient des moulins de polders qui utilisaient l'énergie éolienne pour actionner de grosses pompes destinées à assécher le sol.

ロッテルダムの近くでライン川は二股に分かれ、その北側の支流のレーク川の辺りに１９の風車が見られる。これは粉をひくための風車ではなく、風の力を使ってポンプをまわし、陸の水を汲み出すための低地用風車であった。

It was near Breda, close to the Belgian border, that the uprising against the Spaniards began in 1566, and with it the struggle for the freedom of the Netherlands. The old town centre is dominated by the basilica, the Grote Kerk, with its 97-metre high tower. The 15th century castle was built by the Nassau family, the ancestors of the House of Orange.

In der nahe der belgischen Grenze gelegenen Stadt Breda begann 1566 die Erhebung der Niederlande gegen die Spanier und damit der Freiheitskampf. Beherrschend im alten Stadtzentrum steht die Basilika, die Grote Kerk, mit einem 97 Meter hohen Turm. Schon im 15. Jahrhundert bauten die Nassauer, die Stammfamilien der Oranier, in Breda das heute noch bestehende Schloß.

C'est à Breda, située près de la frontière belge, que les Pays-Bas se soulevèrent contre les Espagnols en 1566, commençant ainsi la guerre d'Indépendance. Le cœur de la vieille-ville est dominée par la basilique dite Grote Kerk, flanquée d'un clocher de 97 mètres. Les Nassau, dont est issue la famille d'Orange, construisirent le château au 15e siècle.

ベルギーとの国境の近くの町、ブレダで、1566年スペインとの戦い、すなわち自由戦争が始まった。古い町の中心には97メートルの塔のバシリカ、グローテ・ケルクがある。既に15世紀には、オラニエ家の本家のナッサウアー家はブレダに城を健城、その城は今も残っている。

In the very west of North Brabant, at the eastern end of the Oosterschelde inlet, a former estuary branch of the Schelde, we find the town of Bergen-op-Zoom. The 15th century Stadhuis on the market-place with its art treasures is worth a visit, as is the Grote Kerk with its tower. On a clear day you can see Antwerp from the top.

Ganz im Westen von Noord-Brabant liegt im innersten Bereich der Osterschelde, einem alten Mündungsarm der Schelde, Bergen op Zoom. Am Markt lohnt das aus dem 15. Jahrhundert stammende Stadhuis mit seinen Kunstschätzen ebenso einen Besuch wie der Turm der Grote Kerk. Von seiner Höhe aus kann man bei klarem Wetter bis Antwerpen sehen.

Bergen op Zoom s'étend à l'ouest du Brabant-Septentrional sur l'Escaut oriental, un vieux bras de l'Escaut, appelé Schelde en néerlandais. Situé sur la place du Marché, l'hôtel de ville du 15e siècle renferme de belles œuvres d'art. Du haut du clocher de l'église, on découvrira une vue splendide jusqu'à Anvers par beau temps.

北ブラバント地方の最西端、オーストスケルデ川の一番奥まった処で、昔のスケルデ川の河口にベルゲン・オプ・ゾームがある。15世紀に建てられた市場広場にある市庁舎には芸術品などもあり、見るに値する。また、グローテ・ケルクの塔に登るのもいいだろう。そこから天気のいい日にはアントワープまで見える。

The Zeeland island of Walcheren on the northern shore of the Westerschelde is often called the garden of Holland. The old ship-building town of Vlissingen (Flushing), situated on its south coast, has grown into a modern industrial town and port. Its chief importance is as the port for ferry services to Sheerness in England.

Die seeländische Insel Walcheren am Nordufer der Westerschelde gelegen wird oft der Garten Hollands genannt. An ihrer Südküste ist die alte Schiffsbauerstadt Vlissingen heute eine moderne Industrie- und Hafenstadt geworden. Vor allem ist sie wichtig als Fährhafen für die Verbindung zum englischen Sheerness.

L'île de Walcheren qui s'étend devant la rive nord de l'Escaut occidental, est souvent appelée le jardin des pays-Bas. Située sur sa côte sud, l'ancienne cité de Vlissingen, réputée pour ses constructions navales, est devenue une ville portuaire et industrielle moderne. C'est de son port notamment que partent les ferry-boats vers Sheerness en Angleterre.

ゼーランド州の島、ワルケレンは西スケルデ川の北岸にあり、オランダの庭と呼ばれている。その南岸には、昔の造船の町、今の工業、港湾都市プリシンヘンがある。特にイギリスのシェールネスへのフェリーポートとして重要。

MIDDELBURG, Walcheren - Zeeland

In former times Walcheren was a popular refuge for all kinds of artists. Today the seaside resorts of Westkapelle, Domburg and Oostkapelle are popular destinations for summer holidaymakers. The capital of the island and province of Zeeland is Middelburg, The little town of Veere has, in recent years, become an important watersports centre.

Walcheren war in früheren Zeiten ein beliebtes Refugium für Künstler jeder Art. Heute sind die Küstenorte Westkapelle, Domburg und Oostkapelle beliebte Urlaubsziele sommerlicher Badegäste. Hauptstadt der Insel wie der Provinz Seeland ist Middelburg. Am Ufer des Veerse Meeres wurde das Städtchen Veere in den letzten Jahren zu einem wichtigen Wassersportzentrum.

Autrefois, Walcheren était un refuge très apprécié des artistes. Les villages côtiers de Westkapelle, Domburg et Oostkapelle sont aujourd'hui des lieux de villégiatures très fréquentés, surtout en été. Middelburg est la ville principale de l'île ainsi que de la province Zélande. La localité de Veere, située sur les bords du Veerse Meer, est devenue un centre important de sports nautiques.

ワルケレンは昔は色々な芸術家の避難所であった。今では海岸の町、ウェストカペレ、ドームブルグ、オーストカペレは特にドイツ人のよく行く夏の休暇地となっている。この島の首都でもあり、ゼーランド州の首都でもあるのがミデルブルグ。昔は裕福な商業中心地であったが、今はその面影はない。

VEERE / Walcheren - Zeeland ▷

The Zeeland bridge over the Ooster-schelde is over 5 kilometres long. It links the islands of Walcheren and Schouwen Duiveland. The main centre on the latter island is the little medieval town of Zierikzee, whose three old town gates still give the place a feeling of seclusion. – This is where the first tour on our pictorial journey ends.

Mehr als 5 Kilometer lang ist die Seelandbrücke über die Osterschelde. Sie verbindet die Inseln Walcheren und Schouwen Duiveland. Wichtigster Ort auf dieser Insel ist das mittelalterliche Städtchen Zierikzee, dem seine drei alten Stadttore immer noch die Atmosphäre der Abgeschlossenheit vermitteln. – Hier endet die erste Tour der Farbbildreise durch Holland.

Le pont de Zélande qui franchit l'Escaut oriental, mesure plus de 5 km. Il relie les îles Walcheren et Schouwen-Duiveland. La localité principale est la petite ville médiévale de Zierikzee qui, cernée de trois portes anciennes, semble encore enfermée dans ses murs. – C'est ici que s'achève le premier circuit de notre voyage photographique à travers la Hollande.

5キロ以上にもわたって、オースタースケルデ川にゼーランドブリッジが架かっている。この橋はワルシェレン島とショヴェ・デューヴェランドとを結んでいる。この島の重要な処は小さな町、ツィーリックゼーであり、3つの市の要塞門があり、市が外と遮断されていた雰囲気がうかがえる。
これでオランダのカラーの写真の旅、第1ツアーを終わる。

North of Amsterdam, on the shores of the southern part of the Ijsselmeer, known as the Markermeer, are two of the most popular destinations in Holland, the island of Marken and the little town of Volendam. Volendam is an old fishing village and, alongside the modern yachts and excursion boats, it is still the fishing boats that shape the atmosphere of the harbour.

Im Norden von Amsterdam liegen am Ufer des Markermeer genannten südlichen Teils des Ijsselmeeres zwei der meistbesuchten Orte Hollands, die Insel Marken und das Städtchen Volendam. Volendam ist ein altes Fischerdorf, und noch immer bestimmen neben den modernen Jachten und Ausflugsbooten der Touristen die Fischerboote das Bild des kleinen Hafens.

Deux des endroits les plus visités de Hollande, l'île Marken et la petite ville de Volendam au nord d'Amsterdam, se trouvent dans la partie sud de l'Ijsselmeer appelée Markermeer. Volendam est un vieux village de pêcheurs. Aujourd'hui encore, les bateaux de pêche qui rapportent surtout des anguilles, côtoient les yachts élégants et les bateaux de croisière pour touristes dans le port.

アイセル湖の南のマルケン湖にオランダで一番訪問客が多いといわれる処が2ヵ所ある。マルケン島と小さな町フォレンダムである。フォレンダムは古い漁村、今は近代的なヨットや観光船も見られるが、それと並んで漁船も見られ、特にフォレンダムの漁師が釣ったうなぎが運ばれてくる光景はここの港らしさをかもしだしている。

VOLENDAM / Noord-Holland

Here the fishermen of Volendam land their catches of eels. Volendam and Marken are two places in Holland where the lovely old traditional costumes and clogs are still in everyday use today. Here and there you can stand and watch a Klompenmacher, a clog-maker, at his work.

VOLENDAM / Noord-Holland

Hier werden vor allem die von Volendamer Fischern gefangenen Aale angelandet. Volendam und Marken gehören zu den holländischen Orten, in denen auch im Alltagsleben heute noch die schönen alten Trachten und Holzschuhe getragen werden. Hier und da kann man auch noch einem Klompenmacher, einem Holzschuhschnitzer, bei der Arbeit zuschauen.

VOLENDAM / Noord-Holland

Volendam et Marken sont deux des endroits en Hollande où les habitants portent encore de beaux costumes folkloriques et des sabots de bois dans la vie quotidienne. Ici et là, on peut encore observer un sabotier dans son atelier.

フォレンダム

フォレンダムとマルケン島の人々は、今でも日常に美しい昔の民族衣装を着、木靴をはいて生活している。あちらこちらで、靴職人が木靴を削って仕事をしている風景が見られる。

North of Volendam is little Edam. What automatically springs to mind when you hear that name is of course cheese. In fact all the cheese produced in this region, the so-called Waterland, is called Edam. It comes as no surprise that the old cheese weighbridge in Edam is still one of the most important buildings in this pleasant little town.

Nördlich an Volendam schließt sich das kleine Edam an. Wer würde da nicht sofort an Käse denken? Tatsächlich werden alle in dieser Gegend, dem sogenannten Waterland, hergestellten Käse kurzerhand Edamer genannt. Verständlicherweise ist die alte Käsewaage in Edam immer noch eines der wichtigsten Gebäude in dem freundlichen Städtchen.

La ville d'Edam, située au nord de Volendam, évoque immédiatement le fromage du même nom. En fait, tous les fromages fabriqués dans cette région dite «Waterland» s'appellent Edam. Un des édifices principaux de la localité paisible est l'ancien édifice du poids-public où les fromages sont encore pesés.

フォレンダムの北に小さな町、エダムが続く。すぐチーズを思い浮かべない者がいるだろうか。確かにウォーターランドと呼ばれるこの地方でつくられたチーズは、全て単にエダマーといわれる。もちろんエダムにある古いチーズ計量所はこの町の一番重要な建物の一つである。

Drawbridges cross the canals, through which the waters of the Ijsselmeer wash into the town. It's not a bad idea to combine a visit to the little cheese town with a boat trip along the canal to the Ijsselmeer. But beforehand, you should that a look at the pretty gabled houses in Edam and listen to the oldest carillon in the whole of Holland.

Zugbrücken überqueren die Kanäle, durch die das Wasser vom Ijsselmeer hereindringt. Es ist nicht die schlechteste Idee einen Besuch der kleinen Käsestadt mit einem Bootsausflug über den Kanal zum Ijsselmeer hinaus zu verbinden. Vorher aber sollte man sich die hübschen alten Giebelhäuser vom Edam anschauen und das älteste Glockenspiel ganz Hollands anhören.

Des ponts mobiles franchissent les canaux où coule l'eau de l'Ijsselmeer. Une jolie excursion est de combiner une excursion par le canal sur l'Ijsselmeer avec un arrêt dans la petite ville du fromage qui a en outre de très belles maisons à pignons et le plus ancien carillon de Hollande à offrir à ses visiteurs.

アイセル湖から流れる運河の上を鉄道が走っている。この小さなエダムの町からボートで運河を通ってアイセル湖に　行ってみるのも悪くない。ボートからエダムのかわいい、古い切り妻壁の家を眺めたり、オランダで一番古い鐘の音を聴くのもいいだろう。

The chief town of West Frieslandhas always been Hoorn, a little port on the Ijsselmeer. The 17th century townscape has been largely preserved. "Hoofdtoren" is the name of the old tower in the harbour. The southernmost tip of South America is named after the town, and it was from here that Jan Pieterszoon Coen set off and discovered Indonesia.

Hauptstadt Westfrieslands ist seit altersher Hoorn, ein Hafenstädtchen am Ijsselmeer, das sich das Bild des 17. Jahrhunderts weitgehend bewahrt hat. „Hoofdtoren", heißt der alte Turm am Hafen jener Stadt, die der Südspitze Südamerikas den Namen gab. Von Hoorn aus fuhr einst Jan Pieterszoon Coen aus und entdeckte Indonesien.

Hoorn est depuis toujours la capitale de l'ouest de la Frise. La petite ville portuaire de l'Ijsselmeer qui a conservé sa physionomie du 17e siècle a donné son nom à la pointe sud de l'Amérique du Sud. Sa pittoresque vieille tour sur le port s'appelle «Hoofdtoren». C'est de Hoorn que Jan Pieterszoon Cœn partit autrefois pour aller découvrir l'Indonésie.

ウェストフリースランドの首都は、アイセル湖畔にある、１７世紀の面影を残している小さな港町、ホールンである。この町の港には、南アメリカの最南端から名前をとった「ホーフト・トーレン」という古い塔がある。このホーレンから、かつてヤン・ピータースゾーン・ケーンが出航し、インドネシアを発見した。

The port of Enkhuizen is situated at the point where the province of North Holland juts furthest east into the Ijsselmeer. The town flourished in the 18th century thanks to a branch of the United East India Company. The Pepper House, the only warehouse from that period that has been preserved, houses the Zuider Zee Museum.

Wo Nordholland am weitesten nach Osten in das Ijsselmeer vorspringt, liegt die Hafenstadt Enkhuizen. Vor allem im 18. Jahrhundert blühte die Stadt dank einer Niederlassung der Vereinigten Ostindischen Kompanie. Im Pfefferhaus, dem einzigen Lagerhaus, das von dieser Kompanie erhalten blieb, kann man das Zuiderseemuseum anschauen.

La ville portuaire d'Enkhuisen est située à l'est de la Hollande-Septentrionale, sur la partie de la province qui pénètre le plus profondément dans l'Ijsselmeer. La ville a surtout connu la prospérité au 18e siècle grâce à un comptoir de la Compagnie des Indes Orientales. La «Maison du poivre», unique entrepôt conservé de la compagnie, abrite aujourd'hui le musée de Zuidersee.

北ホーランド州の最東端、アイセル湖に突き出ている処にあるのが、港町エンク州ハイゼン。18世紀には統一東インド会社がここに支店を置いたため、栄えた。この会社で残っているたった一つの倉庫である胡椒ハウスに南海洋博物館がある。

The old fishing village of Den Helder, on the northern tip of North Holland, was fortified by Napoleon like a Gibraltar of the North. Located between the Waddenzee and the open North Sea, Den Helder is the biggest naval base in the Netherlands and is still an important fishing port. The ferry service to the island of Texel starts from here.

Als Gibraltar des Nordens hat Napoleon das damalige Fischerdorf Den Helder in der Nordspitze Nordhollands befestigt. Den Helder zwischen Nordsee und Wattenmeer gelegen ist heue der größte Kriegshafen der Niederlande und immer noch ein wichtiger Fischereihafen. Von hier aus setzt man mit der Fähre über zur Insel Texel.

Situé à la pointe nord de la Hollande-Septentrionale, l'ancien village de pêcheurs a été fortifié sous Napoléon qui voulait en faire le Gibraltar du Nord. Le Helder qui s'étend entre la mer du Nord et la mer des Watten, est aujourd'hui le plus grand port de guerre des Pays-Bas, mais aussi un port de pêche important. C'est d'ici que les ferry-boats partent pour l'île de Texel.

北のギブラルタルとしてナポレオンは、北ホランド州の最北端の、当時の漁村、デン・ヘルダーの町を固めた。北海とワーデン海の間にあるデン・ヘルダーは今もオランダで一番大きい軍用港であると同時に重要な漁業港でもある。ここからフェリーでテクセル島へ渡れる。

The island of Texel, with an area of 18,600 hectares, is the southernmost of the West Frisian islands and the home of innumerable sheep. The island is a popular bathing resort in the summer. Texel holds a special attraction for birdwatchers. Many different species of seabird can be seen on guided tours through the extensive nature reserves.

Die 18 600 Hektar große Insel Texel, südlichste der Westfriesischen Inseln ist Heimat unzähliger Schafe. Im Sommer wird sie gerne als Ziel für einen Strandurlaub besucht. Es sind vor allem Vogelfreunde, die es immer wieder nach Texel zieht, kann man doch bei geführten Wanderungen durch die großen Vogelschutzgebiete viele Seevögel kennenlernen.

Texel qui a une superficie de 18 600 hectares est l'île la plus au sud de l'Archipel frison occidental. Elle est l'habitat de grands troupeaux de moutons et possèdent de belles plages qui attirent de nombreux vacanciers en été. L'île est également très appréciée des amateurs d'ornithologie qui découvriront de nombreux oiseaux marins lors de visites guidées dans les nombreuses colonies d'oiseaux protégées.

１万８千６百ヘクタールのヘクセル島は、ウェストフリースランドにある島のうちで、一番南にあり、数え切れないほどの羊がいる。夏には海岸で休暇を過ごす人々で賑わう。特に、愛鳥家の中はガイドつきで島歩きをし、海鳥を見ようと何度もこのテクセル島にやってくる人がいる。

The Frisian island of Ameland is about 20 kilometres long and 5 kilometres wide. The ferry service, which links Nes, the main settlement on the island, with Holwerd on the Frisian mainland, crosses the area of mud flats known as the Waddenzee. The Waddenzee is a unique, very sensitive natural environment, also valued as a walking area in the summer.

Rund 20 Kilometer lang und 5 Kilometer breit ist die friesische Insel Ameland. Von Holwerd an der friesischen Festlandküste verkehrt das Fährschiff nach Nes, dem Hauptort der Insel durch das Wattenmeer. Dieses Wattenmeer ist ein eigenartiger, sensibler Lebensraum, der im Sommer auch als Wandergebiet geschätzt wird.

Ameland, île de l'Archipel frison occidental, a environ 20 km de long et 5 km de large et est séparée de la Frise par la mer des Watten. Un ferry-boat relie Holwerd sur le continent à Nes, la localité principale de l'île. Les Watten sont un écosystème unique et fragile que l'on peut explorer à pied en été.

約２０キロの長さ、５キロの幅のフリース地方の島がアメラント。オランダ本土のホルヴェルトから島の中心地ネスまで、ワーデン海にフェリーが通っている。夏には、浅瀬の泥沼歩きの格好の場所として知られているこのワーデン海は、独特で、敏感な島ともいえる。

But walkers need to be in good physical shape and the tide charts must be very strictly observed. Woe betide the unsuspecting or foolhardy walker who is out too late and is caught by the rising tide. Going out on your own or without an experienced guide can be fatal.

Doch solche Wanderungen auf dem Schlickboden verlangen gute Kondition und peinlich genaue Beachtung des Gezeitenkalenders. Wehe dem ahnungslosen oder leichtsinnigen Wattwanderer, der zu spät unterwegs ist und vom auflaufenden Wasser, der Flut, eingeholt wird. Alleine oder ohne erfahrenen Führer sind Wattwanderungen lebensgefährlich.

Mais il faut avoir une bonne condition physique et observer scrupuleusement les heures de marées avant de s'aventurer sur les vastes étendues de vase et de limon. Le randonneur imprudent ou qui s'est attardé, risque d'être surpris par l'arrivée soudaine de la mer. Les promenades dans la mer des Watten sont dangereuses si l'on part seul ou sans guide expérimenté.

この泥沼歩きをするには、ベスト・コンディションと正確な時間の読みが必要である。何も知らずに、気軽に浅瀬の泥沼歩きを始め、途中で遅れてしまうと水かさが増し、満潮になってしまう。一人でや、経験者のガイドなしに泥沼歩きをするのは、非常に危険である。

When it was completed in 1932, the 30-kilometre-long dike between North Holland and Friesland separated the Zuider Zee off from the North Sea. Since then it has been a huge freshwater-fed inland lake, known today as the Ijsselmeer. The construction of the dam was one the most gigantic projects in the Dutch struggle against the sea.

Durch den 1932 fertiggestellten 30 Kilometer langen Abschlußdeich zwischen Nordholland und Friesland wurde die Zuidersee von der Nordsee getrennt. Seitdem ist sie ein riesiger ausgesüsster Binnensee, den man heute Ijsselmeer nennt. Der Bau dieses Deiches war eines der gigantischsten Projekte im Kampf der Holländer gegen das Meer.

La digue de fermeture longue de 30 km qui s'étend entre la Hollande-Septentrionale et la Frise fut construite en 1932 et sépare la Zuidersee de la Mer du Nord. L'immense bassin d'eau dessalée est appelé aujourd'hui Ijsselmeer (lac d'Yssel). La construction de cette digue fut l'un des projets gigantesques des Hollandais dans leur lutte contre la mer.

北ホーラント州とフリースラント州を結ぶ30キロにも渡る堤防が１９３２年に完成したことによって、南海と北海が分離されてしまった。それ以来、今日アイセル海と呼ばれる巨大な内海が出来上がった。この堤防建設はオランダ人が行った海対策のうち、最も膨大なプロジェクトだったといえよう。

Sneek is one of the first places you reach when you come off the dam to Friesland. The little town is the centre of the Frisian lakes area and so, not surprisingly, attracts a lot of watersports fans. Particularly worth seeing are the Waterpoort, the town gate dating from 1631 with its twin towers, the town hall and the Frisian Seafaring Museum.

Sneek ist einer der ersten friesischen Orte, die man erreicht, kommt man über den Abschlußdeich nach Friesland. Die kleine Stadt ist Mittelpunkt des friesischen Seengebietes und zieht entsprechend viele Wassersportler an. Besonders sehenswert sind, das doppeltürmige Stadttor von 1631, das Ratshaus und das Friesische Schifffahrtsmuseum.

Sneek est une des premières localités frisonnes que l'on traverse en arrivant en Frise par la digue de fermeture. La petite ville située au cœur de la région des lacs frisons est très fréquentée des amateurs de sports nautiques. A voir sont la Waterpoort, porte à deux tours datent de 1631 et le musée frison de la Navigation.

堤防を渡り、フリースラント州に入って最初に来る町の一つがスネークである。この小さな町はフリース地方の湖水地帯の中心であり、ウォータースポーツ愛好家がよく訪れる。特に見所といえば、ウォーターポート、1631年に建てられた二本の塔のある市の要塞門、市庁舎フリージアンの船の博物館。

The old capital of the province of Friesland, Leeuwarden, is the centre of an area where people speak Frisian as their mother tongue. Children learn it as a second language at school, too. In the Frisian Museum in Leeuwarden you can learn about the way of life of the Frisians, who are quite different from other Dutch people.

Die alte Hauptstadt der Provinz Friesland, Leeuwarden, ist Mittelpunkt einer Landschaft, in der die Menschen als Muttersprache friesisch sprechen. Auch in der Schule lernen die Kinder diese Sprache als zweite Sprache. Vom Leben der Friesen, die so ganz anders sind als die anderen Niederländer, berichtet das Friesische Museum in Leeuwarden.

Leeuwarden, la vieille capitale de la province de la Frise, s'étend au cœur d'une région dont les habitants parlent le frison, leur langue maternelle, qui est enseignée en deuxième langue dans les écoles. Une visite au musée frison de Leeuwarden fera découvrir la vie et les traditions des Frisons qui sont très différents des autres Hollandais.

フリースラント州の首都、レーワルデンは、景色の奇麗なところである。ここでは母国語としてフリース語を使っている。学校でも子供達は、この言葉を第二国語として習う。フリース人の生活が、
ほかのオランダ人と全く異なるということは、レーワルデンにあるフリース博物館に行くとよくわかる。

Groningen in the northwest of the Netherlands has made a name for itself for some years now with its town planning. Cars were banned from the centre of Groningen long before they were in other Dutch towns, and as a general policy the old parts of the city were gradually restored, rather than cleared and rebuilt with modern new buildings.

Groningen im Nordosten der Niederlande macht schon seit Jahren wegen der hier betriebenen Stadtplanungen von sich reden. Lange bevor man in anderen Städten Hollands so weit war, wurden die Autos aus dem Zentrum Groningens verbannt, suchte man die Stadt Stück für Stück zu sanieren anstatt alte Bausubstanz durch moderne Neubauten zu ersetzen.

Située au nord-est des Pays-Bas, la ville de Groningue fait parler d'elle depuis quelques années en raison de l'urbanisme qui y est pratiqué. Les voitures y ont été bannies du centre-ville avant toutes les autres villes de Hollande. On y a réhabilité peu à peu les quartiers plutôt que de remplacer les constructions anciennes par des immeubles modernes.

オランダの北東にあるフローニンヘンは、かなり前からここで施行されている都市計画で世間を騒がせている。ここでは、オランダの他の都市がやり始めるずっと前から、車をフローニンヘンの町の中心から締め出し、町にある古い建物を一軒一軒新しい建物にと改築していった。

GIETHOORN / Overijssel

The village of Giethoorn in the middle of the "land of water", the western part of the province of Overijssel near the Ijsselmeer, has often been called the Venice of the North. Canals criss-cross the village and the surrounding countryside, extending as far as the Giethoornse Meer, an inland lake, like all the stretches of water in Holland called "Meer". Here the cows are still ferried to the meadows by boat.

GIETHOORN / Overijssel

Als Venedig des Nordens wurde das Dorf Giethoorn oft bezeichnet. Es liegt im Mittelpunkt des „Land des Wassers" genannten westlichen Teils der Provinz Overijssel nahe dem Ijsselmeer. Nach allen Seiten durchziehen Kanäle das Dorf und die Umgebung bis hin zum Giethoornse Meer, das ein Binnensee ist. Hier werden Kühe zum Weidewechsel mit dem Boot befördert.

GIETHOORN / Overijssel

Le village de Giethoorn est souvent décrit comme la Venise du Nord. Il s'étend au cœur du «pays de l'eau» ainsi qu'on appelle la partie occidentale de la province d'Overijssel qui borde l'Ijsselmeer. Un réseau de canaux sillonne le village et la campagne jusqu'à la Giethoornse Meer qui est un lac comme tous les plans d'eau appelés «meer» en Hollande. Même le bétail est transporté ici au pâturage par bateau.

ヒートホールン／オーファルアイセル州

この村は、北のベニスといわれる。ここはアイセル湖の近くで、「水の国」といわれるオーファルアイセル州の西部の中心である。四方八方にと運河が流れ、それがヒートホールン海に流れて、内海となっている。ドレンテ州では、牛を牧場から他の牧場に移すのにボートを使っている。

The old town of Kampen, on the estuary of the Ijssel into the Ijsselmeer, is well worth a visit, with many well preserved historic buildings. Especially noteworthy among them is the Broederpoort with its twin towers, one of the medieval city gates. Kampen lies opposite Flevoland. The whole area is land reclaimed from the Ijsselmeer.

Kampen an der Mündung der Ijssel ins Ijsselmeer ist eine sehenswerte alte Stadt mit vielen gut erhaltenen historischen Gebäuden. Unter ihnen fällt besonders die doppeltürmige Broederpoort auf, eines der mittelalterlichen Stadttore. Kampen gegenüber liegt Flevoland. Die gesamte Landschaft wurde durch Eindeichung dem Ijsselmeer abgewonnen.

Kampen est située à l'embouchure de l'Ijssel dans l'Ijsselmeer. La jolie ville ancienne a conservé de nombreux édifices historiques dont la Broederpoort à deux tours, une des portes médiévales de la cité. La province de Flevoland s'étend en face de Kampen. Ce polder a été gagné sur l'Ijsselmeer par endiguement.

アイセル川がアイセル海にそそぎ込む河口にあるカムペンは、沢山のよく保存されている歴史的な建物があり、見る価値がある。そのうちで特に2本の塔のある中世の市の要塞門のブレーデルポールトが目立つ。カムペンの反対側がフレフォラント州である。アイセル海に堤防がかけられたので、ここの景観がすっかり変わってしまった。

Zwolle, the capital of the province of Overijssel, was a rich Hansa town in the Middle Ages. Visitors shouldn't miss the magnificent interior of the 15th century town hall. A particularly striking building is the Sassenpoort, the Saxon Gate with its five towers built in the year 1408.

Zwolle, die Hauptstadt der Provinz Overijssel, hat eine Vergangenheit als reiche Hansestadt hinter sich. Im Rathaus aus dem 15. Jahrhundert sollte man sich den prächtigen Schöffensaal anschauen. Ein besonders markantes Bauwerk der Stadt ist die im Jahre 1408 erbaute fünftürmige Sassenpoort, das „Sachsentor".

Zwolle, la capitale de la province d'Overijssel, possède le riche passé d'une ville ayant appartenu à la ligue marchande de la Hanse. Dans l'hôtel de ville du 15e siècle, on peut admirer une Salle des Echevins splendide. Un autre édifice intéressant de la ville est la Sassenpoort à cinq tours datant de 1408, appelée la «Porte des Saxons».

オーファルアイセル州の州都であるズウォレは、過去には裕福なハンザ都市であった。市庁舎には、15世紀に造られた豪華な議会ホールもある。特にこの町で見るべき建築物は、1408年に建築された「ザクセン門」とよばれる5本の塔のあるサッセンポールトである。

In 1685 William of Orange III had a castle built as a hunting seat near the village of Apeldoorn. The architect was the Frenchman Daniel Marot. Before it was turned into a museum in 1972, Het Loo had served as a retirement home for the Dutch Queen Wilhemina. The castle's French gardens are quite unique in Holland.

1685 ließ sich Willem III. von Oranien von dem französischen Architekten Daniel Marot nahe dem Dorf Apeldoorn ein Jagdschloß bauen, Het Loo. Bevor es 1972 als Museum eingerichtet wurde, hatte es der holländischen Königin Wilhelmina als Alterssitz gedient. Einzigartig in Holland sind die französischen Gärten des Schlosses.

Le château de chasse Het Loo qui se dresse près du village d'Apeldoorn, fut construit en 1685 par l'architecte français Daniel Marot pour Guillaume III d'Orange. Il fut la dernière résidence de la reine Wilhelmina avant d'être transformé en musée en 1972. Les jardins à la française du château sont uniques en Hollande.

１６８５年、オラニエ家のウィレム３世は、フランスの設計家のダニエル・マローにアペルドールンの近くに狩猟用の城ヘート・ローを建てさせた。この城の庭は、オランダで唯一つのフランス庭園である。

Amersfoort lies in the middle of sandy forest and heathland. The most prominent monuments include the stately Koppelspoort spanning the Eem, built around 1400. The Kamperbinnenpoort also gives the city, the second largest in the province of Utrecht, a medieval touch, as do the old houses.

In einer sandigen Wald- und Heidelandschaft liegt Amersfoort. Zu den charakteristischsten Bauwerken der Stadt gehört die bereits um 1400 gebaute stattliche Koppelsport, die die Eem überspannt. Auch die Kamperbinnenpoort gibt dieser zweitgrößten Stadt der Provinz Utrecht noch etwas Mittelalterliches, ebenso wie der alte Häuserring.

Amersfoort s'étend dans une région au sol sableux de forêts et de landes. Un des édifices caractéristiques de la ville est la Koppelspoort, une porte majestueuse datant de 1400, qui se dresse au-dessus de l'Eem. La Kamperbinnenpoort ainsi que les anciennes rues apportent également une touche médiévale à la deuxième ville de la province d'Utrecht.

砂地の森やヒースの生えている荒れ野にアーメルスフォールトはある。この町の性格をよくあらわしている建築物は、1400年に建てられたエームの上にかかっている威厳あるコッペルスポールトである。カムパービンネンポールトや古い家が建ち並ぶムールホイゼンも、このユトレヒト州二番目に大きな町に中世の面影を注いている。

The layout and townscape of Naarden between Amersfoort and Amsterdam can only be described as unique. It was built in the shape of a star and surrounded with moats, following designs by Vauban, the French master-architect of fortifications. Naarden has remained unchanged since 1685 and is the best preserved set of fortifications in Holland.

Anlage und Stadtbild von Naarden zwischen Amersfoort und Amsterdam muß man als einzigartig bezeichnen. Nach dem System der Festungen des französischen Festungsbaumeisters Vauban wurde Naarden sternförmig angelegt und mit sternförmigen Wassergräben umgeben. Seit 1685 blieb Naarden unverändert und ist heute die besterhaltene Festung ganz Hollands.

Naarden, située entre Amersfoort et Amsterdam, a une physionomie unique en Hollande. La ville a été construite en forme d'étoile et entourée de fossés épousant cette configuration selon le modèle des fortifications de Vauban. Naarden n'a pas changé d'aspect depuis 1685 et est aujourd'hui la ville fortifiée la mieux conservée du pays.

アーメルスフォールトとアムステルダムの間にあるナールデンの建物や景観は特別のものである。フランスの要塞建築主任であるファウバンの要塞システムで造られたこのナールデンは、星形に造られ、星形に堀が掘られている。1685年から、ナールデンは変わっておらず、今日ではオランダで最もよく保存されている要塞である。

UTRECHT / Prov. Utrecht

Utrecht, the fourth largest city in Holland, is both the country's most important communications centre, and a dreamy old town. The cathedral, towering up above the old city and the canals below, is about 600 years old. Utrecht offers a unique combination of the historical and the avant-garde, like no other city or town in Holland.

UTRECHT / Prov. Utrecht

Die viertgrößte Stadt Hollands ist einerseits der wichtigste Verkehrsknotenpunkt des Landes und gleichzeitig eine verträumte, alte Stadt. Rund 600 Jahre alt ist der Dom, der die von Grachten durchzogene Altstadt überragt. Nirgendwo in Holland zeigt eine Stadt so wohlerhaltene und gleichzeitig so avantgardistische Züge wie Utrecht.

UTRECHT / Prov. Utrecht

Utrecht, la quatrième ville de Hollande est le nœud de communication principal du pays tout en présentant l'atmosphère d'une paisible cité ancienne. La cathédrale, construite il y a 600 ans, domine la vieille-ville sillonnée de canaux. Nulle autre agglomération hollandaise n'est aussi bien conservée tout en présentant de nombreux aspects avant-gardistes.

ユトレヒト／ユトレヒト州

オランダで第四番目に大きいこの都市は、この国の一番重要な交通の接点でもあり、同時に夢のような古い町でもある。運河が流れる旧市街にそびえ立つ大聖堂は、約６００年も前の建物この町程よく保存され、同時に前衛的な町もオランダには他にない。

Arnhem, the capital of Gelderland, the largest Dutch province, is situated on the Neder Rijn, the branch of the Rhine that, further west, is called the Lek. The city was badly destroyed in the Second World War, but has been attractively reconstructed. The open air folk museum close-by is particularly worth a visit.

Am Neder Rijn genannten Rheinarm, der weiter westlich dann Lek genannt wird, liegt Arnheim, die Hauptstadt Gelderlands, der größten holländischen Provinz. Im zweiten Weltkrieg wurde die Stadt stark zerstört, ist jedoch ansprechend wieder aufgebaut. Besonders sehenswert ist das nahe der Stadt gelegene Niederländische Freilichtmuseum.

Arnhem, la capitale de la Gueldre, la plus grande province hollandaise, s'étend sur le Neder Rijn, un bras du Rhin qui prend le nom de Lek un peu plus loin vers l'ouest. La ville a été reconstruite après avoir subi de graves dommages durant la seconde guerre mondiale. A voir tout particulièrement est le musée de plein air des Pays-Bas, situé près d'Arnhem.

ネーダーラインと呼ばれるライン川が枝のように二股に分かれ、もっと西になるとレーク川になる処に、オランダで一番大きな州であるヘルダーラント州の州都、アルンヘムがある。第二次世界大戦でこの町は、かなり破壊されたが、再建されている。　この町の見るべき所として、町の近くにあるネダーラント野外博物館がある。

Nijmegen, situated only a few kilometres from the German border, is like an amphitheatre, the way it has been built on seven hills. The city lies on the River Waal, the larger, more southerly of the two branches into which the Rhine divides near Nijmegen. As long ago as the year 768, Charlemagne built an imperial palace here.

Wie ein Amphitheater baut sich nur wenige Kilometer von der deutschen Grenze entfernt die Stadt Nijmegen, im deutschen Nimwegen genannt, auf sieben Hügeln auf. Die Stadt liegt an der Waal, dem südlichen, größeren der beiden Arme, in die der Rhein sich bei Nijmegen spaltet. Schon 768 gründete Karl der Große hier eine Kaiserpfalz.

Nimègue, située à quelques kilomètres seulement de la frontière allemande, est construite en forme d'amphithéâtre sur sept collines. Elle s'étend sur la Waal, nom donné au plus large des deux bras du Rhin qui se divise aux abords de la ville. Dès 768, Charlemagne avait créé un palais à cet endroit.

ドイツの国境から、ほんの数キロしか離れていない、七つの丘の上に、ドイツ語ではフィームヴェーゲンと呼ばれるナイメーヘンの町が、円形劇場のように造られている。この町は、ナイメーゲンの近くでライン川が、二股に分かれ、その南側のワール川の辺りにある。768年には、カール大帝が皇帝城を建城した。

's-Hertogenbosch, Den Bosch for short, is the centre and capital of the province North Brabant. The famous painter Hieronymus Bosch was born here in 1450. The focal point of the city is the triangular marketplace with the Gothic-Baroque town hall. Rising up behind it is the Cathedral of St. Jan, the most significant medieval church in Holland.

's-Hertogenbosch, auch kurz Den Bosch genannt, ist Mittelpunkt und Hauptstadt der Provinz Nord-Brabant. Hier wurde 1450 der berühmte Maler Hieronymus Bosch geboren. Mittelpunkt der Stadt ist der dreieckige Marktplatz mit dem gotisch-barocken Rathaus, hinter dem sich die Kathedrale St. Jan erhebt, die bedeutendste mittelalterliche Kirche Hollands.

Bois-le-Duc, appelé 's-Hertogenbosch ou Den Bosch en néerlandais, est le chef-lieu de la province du Brabant-Septentrional. Le célèbre peintre Hieronymus Bosch y est né en 1450. Le cœur de la ville est la place du Marché triangulaire avec l'hôtel de ville de styles gothique et baroque, derrière lequel se dresse la cathédrale St. Jan, la plus importante église médiévale du pays.

スヘルトヘンボスは、短縮してデン・ボスといわれているが、北ブラバント州の中心であり、州都でもある。1450年に、画家のイロニイムス・ボスがここで生まれている。町の中心は、ゴチック式、バロック式で建てられた支庁舎のある三角形の市場広場。その後ろには、オランダの最も重要な中世の教会、聖ヤン・カテドラルがある。

MAASTRICHT / Limburg

The province of Limburg extends south along the German border like an elongated appendix. Right down in the south is Maastricht, known in Holland as the city of the good life. The origins of the St. Servatius church date back to the 6th century. The picture shows the Vrithof with the St. Servatius and St. Jans churches.

Wie ein Wurmfortsatz zieht sich die Provinz Limburg lang und schmal an der deutschen Grenze entlang nach Süden. Ganz unten im Süden liegt Maastricht, das in Holland als Stadt des guten Lebens gilt. Die St.-Servatius-Kirche (6. Jhdt.) ist die älteste Kirche Hollands. Das Bild zeigt den Vrithof mit der St.-Servatius-Kirche und St.-Jans-Kirche.

La province du Limbourg, qui a la forme d'un appendice vermiculaire, s'étire en une bande étroite le long de la frontière allemande. Son chef-lieu, Maastricht, est situé tout au sud, sur la Meuse. L'église Saint-Servais date du début du 6e siècle. L'église de St-Servatius (6e siècle) est la plus ancienne de Hollande. L'image montre le Vrithof avec St-Servatius et St-Jans.

盲腸の虫様垂の用に長く細くドイツの国境に沿って南に伸びているのが、リンブルフ州である。その再南端最にあって、、オランダのグット・ライフの町といわれるのがマストリヒト。6世紀の始めにできた聖セルバチウス教会がある。これはオランダで一番古い教会であり、沢山名所があるうちの一つである。写真に見られるのは、ヘウフェルーギャラリーの近代的ショッピングセンターの一部である。